ANCHORED *by* HOPE

Meditations to Calm the Anxious Soul

ELIZABETH M. KELLY

Published by The Word Among Us Press
7115 Guilford Drive, Suite 100
Frederick, Maryland 21704
wau.org

30 29 28 27 26   1 2 3 4 5

ISBN: 978-1-59325-747-7

eISBN: 978-1-59325-748-4

Design by Rose Audette

Library of Congress Control Number: 2026907061

For all those whose hearts have grown weary.
"Wait for the Lord; be strong, and let your heart
take courage; wait for the Lord!"
ℰᴐPsalm 27:14ᴈᴈ

CONTENTS

Opening Epistle

In quietness and in trust shall be your strength.
ℇIsaiah 30:15ℂ

It was as if this verse had searched for me, found me, and then settled on me like a warm blanket. I returned to it again and again in that year with breast cancer. It became a kind of theme song for the season and a constant source of comfort, a tonic to restore calm. I know the Lord gave me that verse as a gift.

If you've had cancer or any serious disease, you know what it's like. Your body becomes a full-time job and there are so many important decisions to be made with no outcomes guaranteed. As much as we might wish it otherwise, medicine is more art than science and nothing is certain.

Our deliberations included: lumpectomy or mastectomy or double mastectomy? Chemotherapy, radiation, pills, nothing? A combination of things? We wondered, will the treatment we choose kick my multiple sclerosis into overdrive? What would insurance cover? Would chemo make me too sick to work? And when my husband got laid off just after I had surgery, we stretched our eyes to heaven and said, "Really? Now?" How in the world would we manage?

Whenever I felt tempted to panic or grow harried, this verse would alight on my heart: "In quietness and in trust shall be your strength" (Isaiah 30:15), and I'd grow calm again, sure, hopeful—not in doctors or outcomes or treatments or the future, but in the Lord who was surely with me in every moment, in every decision, in every bit of suffering, lending it meaning and purpose and power. His power—his redemptive, restorative, transformative power.

Of course, this is exactly what God's word does: it brings the Author of all creation into the room. I say this again and again: the Bible is the only book you will read where every time you do, every time you open its pages, the Author is in the room—alive, breathing, active, aware, and awake to your heart. Of this I am utterly convinced: the Lord desires to accompany us through his word. He longs for us to know him, to know his heart, his loves, his joys, and his sorrows through his holy word.

And it is in this attitude that the verses here have been chosen for our prayer and meditation. Whatever you might be facing, whatever question mark might be hanging over your future or the life of someone you love, God's word can speak to it—God's word can speak to *you*.

My hope is that you won't simply read these passages of Scripture but that you will pray with them and allow them to speak to your heart in the personal and effective way that the Lord does. I've offered a few prompts at the end of each reflection to help you enter God's word. Use them if you find them meaningful, and don't be timid about repetitions. Pray with these verses again and again, throughout the day or over several days' or months' time, and allow God's word to find you, choose you, speak to you, and rest on you like a warm blanket, a soft breeze, a guiding light, a mighty arm, a flowing river, or a sweet incense.

The world may feel dark and foreboding. Sometimes it is exactly that, but God's word is always a lamp to our feet and a light to our path (see Psalm 119:105). Let's join in the prayer of the great prophet Jeremiah: "Your words were found, and I ate them, and your words became to me a joy and the delight of my heart; for I am called by your name, O Lord, God of hosts" (15:16).

I pray that the Lord's word will become alive to you in these pages and speak deeply and personally to your heart.

Float

Be still, and know that I am God!
℘Psalm 46:10℘

My brother showed up with no notice. It was a gorgeous, sunny spring day, and I was outside watering my flowers when he pulled up and got out of his car looking completely exhausted.

I know that his job as rector of a seminary is extremely demanding. He will go for months on end with no more than four hours of sleep each night. I could tell by just looking at him that he needed to disappear for a while.

My plan was to work all day. I had an enormous load of writing due, and I was behind. A few days earlier, my dog had spilled my coffee on my laptop. You can imagine the hours it took to undo that mess. I lost a few more days to unforeseen medical appointments, the excitement of the papal conclave, and unexpected visitors. I needed to work.

My brother asked, "Want to go rent a pontoon?" Inside, I said, "No, I want to work!" But I knew he needed it. To him, I replied, "Absolutely."

We live between two lakes, and there was a pontoon rental place minutes from my front door. We packed water, snacks, and some towels and headed out the door. I also toted along a notebook and some work on my restored laptop, planning to sneak in a little writing if my brother took a well-earned snooze.

But as soon as we stepped onto the pontoon and the crew pushed us off the dock, I knew Jesus wasn't asking me to write this afternoon. Still, I felt a nagging sense of falling further behind.

We toured the lake a bit. It was a glorious day, warm but not humid, sunny but not too hot. It was a weekday so there were very few people on the lake. We headed for the deepest part and dropped anchor. My brother dove in, took a brief swim and then stretched out on a towel to sun like a lizard on a rock. He fell asleep.

I pulled out my laptop and tried to work a little, but the light dancing off the water and that lovely sensation of being adrift on gentle lilting waves overcame any desire to write. In my heart as I took in the glorious day around me, I heard the Lord say, "It's okay, just go ahead and float."

I wanted to resist, but he continued, always so patient with me, "Who do you think gave you all of that good work?"

"You did, Lord," I said.

"Who do you think inspires you with all those good ideas?"

"You do, Father."

"Have I ever let you down?"

"No, Lord."

"Who made all of this glory around you for you to enjoy?"

"You did, Father; you did."

I shut my laptop and stuffed it back in my bag.

It's okay. Some days you need to just go ahead and float.

Ponder this before the Lord

What's your daily routine like? Do you make time to rest with the Lord, really and truly just be with him and relish the world he has created? Can you schedule some time to be still with the Lord this week?

Emptiness

When the wine gave out, the mother of Jesus said to him,
"They have no wine." And Jesus said to her, "Woman,
what concern is that to you and to me? My hour has not
yet come." His mother said to the servants, "Do whatever
he tells you." Now standing there were six stone water jars
for the Jewish rites of purification, each holding twenty or
thirty gallons. Jesus said to them, "Fill the jars with water."
And they filled them up to the brim.
ᏹJohn 2:3-7ᏹ

I remember exactly where I was sitting when the invitation came in: to write an Advent devotional for Blessed Is She, a beautiful young women's apostolate. The topic: hope. I was thrilled.

But I was also in the final stages of chemotherapy. I was bald, exhausted, and weak. Chemo had been very hard, made harder by the fact that I also have multiple sclerosis. Fatigue is already a daily part of life. But with chemo, there were days I could barely get out of bed. I felt completely empty—of energy, ideas, creativity, everything—emptier and more drawn than I had ever felt in my life. So how in the world could I take on a book contract?

I went to Adoration and talked it over with Jesus in the Blessed Sacrament. I told him point-blank, "I have nothing to give." To my surprise, in that moment, he filled me with confidence and joy, hope and ideas. Turns out, Jesus was not afraid of my emptiness. In fact, I think he may have been waiting for it. Just like the stone jars at the wedding feast of Cana, I was just sitting there, empty, waiting for the Lord to fill me. And fill me not just with any old thing, but with water he would transform into "the good wine" (John 2:10). I went to work, praying countless times, "Lord, I know you will give me what I need for this project."

He did—he filled me "up to the brim" and more (John 2:7). The book turned out splendidly and received some of the most overwhelmingly positive feedback of any work I've ever written.

My friends, this is *exactly* how Jesus works. We come to him in our utter need and he touches us, just as we are, and fills our emptiness with life-giving resources. And not only that, but he transforms them into excellence—the best, the good wine.

As terrible as emptiness can feel at times, Jesus is never afraid of it. He might even be waiting for it, allowing the trials that strain us and drain us so that we become still, empty, and available to him for excellent, life-giving collaboration.

Ponder this before the Lord

Are you available? Are you empty? Are you still and ready to be filled, to be touched by the powerful hand of God, to be transformed, to be made excellent, life-giving? Speak to Jesus about any areas of your life where you feel empty.

3

A Father's Embrace

You have a mighty arm;
strong is your hand, high your right hand.
ℬ Psalm 89:13 ℭ

I n my twenties, I worked for an entrepreneur who worked out of his home, which meant I worked from his home, too. I got to know the goings-on of his large family very well. He had seven sons, strapping and boisterous, ranging from grade school to college age, and just one daughter, who was about eleven when I first knew her. She was a precious child with a huge, open heart. She was bubbly and animated and creative. She dearly loved the Lord, and I often looked at her with some apprehension—she was so innocent, I knew the world would be hard on her.

One evening as I was getting ready to leave for the day, the daughter walked in looking downtrodden and stood quietly before her father. He stopped what he was doing and turned all of his attention toward her, looking on her with such profound tenderness.

She had tried out for the school play and had not been selected for any role whatsoever. This clearly had crushed her spirit. And it was surprising, because she seemed to me to be a rather good fit for something dramatic. News of her disappointment had been delivered to my boss earlier in the day by his wife. Now, the daughter stood before her father, her shoulders sunken, her eyes on the floor.

Her father sat quietly. It seemed to me he was arriving, settling into her grief, reverencing it somehow. And then after a moment, he simply said, "It hurts, doesn't it?" With that, his daughter crumpled, falling into his stout arms where she sobbed until her cheeks turned pink and his shirt was soaked with tears and whatnot.

He just held her and let her cry, and in the ways that fathers can do this—I could see it viscerally—he absorbed some of her pain and disappointment. I watched it disappear into the ether and the strength of his confident embrace. The rejection that had threatened to ruin her was beaten down by the overwhelming and completely compelling knowledge that she belonged to him and he *loved* her, *treasured* her.

I have thought of the fatherly genius of this moment many times. How this spoke to my own heart. How safe I am, how welcome to fall into the arms of my Father and have a good, pink-cheeked, tear-soaked-shirt kind of cry when the world is cruel and disappointing. And we know it can be.

And how capable and willing the Father is to absorb my pain and disappointment, to remind me with the strength of his arm, his mighty arm, that nothing the world does to me can rob me of his loving embrace.

Ponder this before the Lord

Is there some pain, some rejection you would allow the Father to take from you, to transform into the knowledge that you are loved by a mighty God? Can you imagine standing before his tender gaze and allowing him to hold you with his strong, loving embrace? Would you allow him to reverence this pain you carry, to enter into it and transform it into the truth that you are precious in his sight?

4

What Hope Must Do

You are a hiding place for me;
you preserve me from trouble.
☙Psalm 32:7❧

When I first started having serious health problems, I got into the habit of praying before every doctor visit and every MRI or mammogram or blood test: "Jesus, I love you more than anything and I'm going to love you forty-five minutes from now when the results come back. I know you love me and nothing in this test is going to change that. So, we're good." It's so elementary as to be embarrassing, but it has always managed to settle my heart. This little habit has a-righted me time and again when I was fearful about the future.

That is what Christian hope does: it radically realigns my relationship to fear, because hope doesn't live in my body or my mind or in an earthly outcome. It cannot be moved by disease or economic collapse. Hope is a gift given by a good and generous God, who in unspeakable love imagined and brought into being the Incarnation: Jesus, the source of all hope. My work is to beg, every single day, for a new infilling of it.

Many "hope imposters" parade through our culture. Pope Benedict XVI wrote so convincingly about the "parody of faith and hope" that leads to an imagined utopia. Too often the desire to get my own way, to have the last word, or to succeed in my own plans dresses up like faith and hope only to be painfully exposed at the first smattering of failure. Hope is not the equivalent of my getting what I want, even when what I want is good: health or stability or peace on earth.

Benedict wrote,

> Man is not the only actor on the stage of history, and that is why death does not have the last word in it. The fact that there is this other person who is active is alone the firm and certain anchor of a hope that is stronger and more real than all the frightfulness of the world.[1]

Check your hope. Is it authentic, rooted in Christ? Or has it been taken over by an unfortunate imposter? To reanchor your hope, to make it "stronger and more real than all the frightfulness of the world," remember that Jesus and his Church will long outlast this moment in history, the pain that feels overwhelming, the struggle that threatens your peace, and whatever fearsome challenge you are facing. He loves you. You're good.

Ponder this before the Lord

Take a "hope inventory." How strong is your hope? Do you need a fresh infusion? Can you rest in the verse above from the psalms until your hope is renewed?

5

Body Fear

[Jesus] said to Simon, "Put out into the deep water and let down your nets for a catch." Simon answered, "Master, we have worked all night long but have caught nothing. Yet if you say so, I will let down the nets." When they had done this, they caught so many fish that their nets were beginning to break.... But when Simon Peter saw it, he fell down at Jesus' knees, saying, "Go away from me, Lord, for I am a sinful man!" For he and all who were with him were amazed at the catch of fish that they had taken; and so also were James and John, sons of Zebedee, who were partners with Simon. Then Jesus said to Simon, "Do not be afraid; from now on you will be catching people." When they had brought their boats to shore, they left everything and followed him.

ം Luke 5:4-6, 8-11 ര

The first symptoms of multiple sclerosis hit me in my twenties. They were vague, menacing, and difficult to diagnose. I wasn't definitively diagnosed for nearly two decades. It wasn't until I went numb from the waist down, but only on the back half of my body—and how weird was that?—that doctors were able to diagnose me. I was relieved. All those odd symptoms, all those years.

It wasn't just my imagination; I didn't need therapy or a vacation. There was actually a disease at work in my body. It was a relief to finally know.

Still, those long years waiting for information schooled me all too well in being afraid of my body.

Then I got cancer. And then six years later, cancer again. My body fear was reignited in a whole new way. Every lump and bump and ache and pain became an opportunity for wonder and worry about the future. But that's no way to live, not for a disciple of Christ.

The first apostles left everything and immediately followed the Lord. Do I have that kind of willingness and energy? To become a disciple of Jesus means a new freedom from attachments, especially the difficult ones. My attachment to my body, the fear and the energy it had taken to manage it through illness, was weighing me down.

In a new way, I sense Jesus inviting me to leave this behind: body fear. I don't need to carry that anymore. I don't need to lug that anxious and ugly "maybe" around for the rest of my life. It hinders me in serving him, in following him, and in finding the joy that it is to be his follower—right now, in this moment.

Some disease may visit me again. That's just the world we live in. But for today, I put down my body fear, and I follow Jesus into the future with a new hope that, as Pope St. John Paul II once said, "It is worth staking everything on Christ."

Ponder this before the Lord

Is Jesus inviting you to follow him in a new way? Is there a fear or worry that hinders you from committing your life to Christ more fully? Can you name it and give it to the Lord, and trust him with it? What would it mean for you to put that fear down and walk into the future with Jesus?

6

Rocks Were Split

From noon on, darkness came over the whole land until three in the afternoon. . . .Then Jesus cried again with a loud voice and breathed his last. At that moment the curtain of the temple was torn in two, from top to bottom. The earth shook, and the rocks were split.
ℬMatthew 27:45, 50-51℞

The day of the funeral had one of the worst summer storms I can recall. A young colleague had lost her second son just two days before he was to be born. One evening, she noticed he seemed too still, that he had stopped moving and kicking and frolicking inside as he usually did just as she settled in at bedtime.

They rushed to the doctor who confirmed it: there was no heartbeat. After two days of utter agony, she gave birth to her stillborn baby boy. He was perfect. There was simply no explanation for why his life was taken before it had barely begun. The loss was unspeakable.

Visitation was held just before the funeral, and there is nothing quite so stark and heartbreaking as an infant's casket. As they sat with their son, candles burning beside him, I hugged my young friends, cried with them, and had nothing whatever to say. I took a seat about midway up the church on the aisle and waited for the service to begin.

I will never forget that Mass: just as the funeral procession began and the two pallbearers began to walk down the aisle carrying their precious consignment between them, the skies opened up with thunder and lightning and pouring rain such as I have rarely seen in my life. It shook the rafters. It drowned out the organ. It was as if the entire world cried out in agony. And it was the first moment I really understood, or at least appreciated, Christ's death on the cross: when the sky grew dark and the temple veil was torn in two, and the earth shook and the rocks were split. Some losses are so great, so momentous, that even the very earth we stand on, the wind and rain, the planets and stars of the heavens, must join in the mourning.

I've always thought of that pounding storm as a gift to my young friends in their loss. How dare the earth be bright and cheery on such a solemn day? And as I left the church, the rain still poured and my young friends sat in the funeral cortege awaiting the trip to the cemetery, the raindrops pounding the cars with unrelenting tears. Nothing could have been more fitting.

Indeed, it seems in his mercy and might, the Creator has made earth and sky and universes not a separate thing, but a brother and sister to his children, something to sing his glory and reveal his beauty. The earth and heavens join in our joy too. The sunrise alone can be a vivid reminder that the Lord is ever near, ever faithful. A sunset can bring peace and an end to a day's toil and suffering. Spring erupts like newfound faith. Fall brings cool color and reminders of the last things, death and eternity.

We share this with the world around us: we were brought into being by a mighty, loving, glorious God.

Ponder this before the Lord

Can you recall a time when the earth and its splendor and majesty spoke to your heart about the Lord? Can you recall a moment when God's creation brought you comfort, solace, or companionship? Speak to him about this.

7

All Things New

The one who was seated on the throne said,
"See, I am making all things new."

Revelation 21:5

A woman approaches me after I've given a talk for a large women's conference. She is small, drawn, and so weary.

She says, "Can I talk to you?" We try to step to the side of the room where it's a bit less frenzied with the kind of chatter and noise that a large conference has.

She looks around a bit sheepishly, almost embarrassed, and then says—no, whispers, "I've never had my own life."

The room is buzzing and I lean in and ask her, "Will you repeat that?"

She says again, "I've never had my own life." This time, I look into her face and there's such deep sorrow and pain there, I can hardly describe it.

She goes on to tell me that she grew up with a brother who had profound special needs. She ended up caring for him because her mother simply couldn't. Her mother, who'd been abandoned by her spouse, suffered with mental illness. The daughter stepped in to care for her brother long into his adult life until she could no longer manage his profound needs. About the time the brother was put into a state-run care home, her mother developed Alzheimer's disease. The woman swiftly moved from attending to her brother to attending to her mother, and neither were easy patients. Her mother was slowly ravaged by the disease another twelve years, all the while being cared for at home by her daughter.

She said it one last time, choking on the words, "I've never had my own life." I thought she might burst into tears, but the swell of the crowd took her aback. She shook her head, looked at the floor, and started for the door. I wanted to run after her, to hold her hand, to look into her eyes and say, "It's never too late. God can redeem all lost time. God will make all things new." I wanted to, but another woman came to tell me that her husband, just thirty-nine years old, had recently died of cancer, leaving her a single mother with several young children. Suddenly, I was caught up in the tale of another sorrow so great, there just aren't words.

Life can be so cruel. Its demands can rise up and overwhelm in an instant. Our life can be taken up—entirely, every ounce, every iota—for the needs of others, so much so that we never have the sense of having chosen a life of our own. It is natural to question, *Could this possibly be the life the Lord intended for me?*

There's no pithy answer to such loss. But I will say, I believe with my entire being that God's word is true. And I claim its promises for these women. I stand in the gap on their behalf and shout to the heavens, "Lord, seated on your throne, remember them. In this moment, I beg you, break in upon their lives in such a way that they know they are seen, they are loved, and that you,

in all your mystery, have a plan for them—for good, for whole-
ness, for joy in you."

And oh yes, I claim these promises for you too.

Ponder this before the Lord

Where in your life would you wish to be made new? Is
there some small step you could take today to invite the
Lord's renewing power into your heart?

8

Who Owns You?

"If the world hates you, be aware that it hated me before it hated you. If you belonged to the world, the world would love you as its own. Because you do not belong to the world, but I have chosen you out of the world—therefore the world hates you."

ɤ John 15:18-19 ɞ

Many years ago, I was invited to speak at a Newman Center that was holding a series of talks for their Lenten season. I was to speak on the role of beauty in the life of faith and how beauty invites us to know the Lord, even in seasons of suffering. We agreed to a date, signed a contract, and I set about preparing.

However, it became clear to me, as I corresponded with the gentleman who'd invited me, that he somehow thought I was very liberal in my faith, anti-Magisterial, very progressive—which I am not. I'm not sure how he got this impression, but it was clear that if I showed up and spoke the way I intended, on the subject I intended, that he was going to be wildly disappointed.

I consulted a colleague on the matter. The director for the Center for Catholic Studies where I worked was a wildly intelligent man of vast experience and diplomacy. We took a walk around the block as I explained my dilemma. I wondered, Should I clarify the error or just show up and be, well . . . disappointing?

Without a moment's hesitation, my colleague said, "I think a little disappointment is called for." It was a breakthrough moment that I will carry with me until the day I die. I was flooded with relief and freedom. Not only was I given permission to be a disappointment, I was even encouraged to be so. And he was, of course, absolutely right: my only task was to be obedient to God's call; the results were completely out of my hands.

I went to the gig and was, in fact, a disappointment to the gentleman who invited me. He picked me up at the airport a few hours before I was to speak. As it became clearer to him who I was and who owned my heart, he grew shorter and shorter, snapping commands at me. As I spoke that evening to a crowd of maybe a hundred, I could see him shrinking in his chair with a faint look of disgust. Furthermore, he did not meet the contracted obligation but shorted me by half the agreed-upon amount without offering any explanation whatsoever.

The rest of the audience was another matter. Many people approached me after my talk to say how much they enjoyed it, and how much they wished that the organizer would bring in more people like me. I chuckled to myself all the way home on the flight. Being a "disappointment" turned out to be rather enjoyable. And this "failure" that I was dreading actually became life-giving.

We could argue that by the cultural standards of his time, Jesus was a failure. Abandoned by his followers in the moment of his greatest need, he met a wretched end in the eyes of those who did not understand who he was and what he was doing. He wasn't building a business; he was building a kingdom. And what people thought about him was completely irrelevant to that mission. He knew he belonged to the Father.

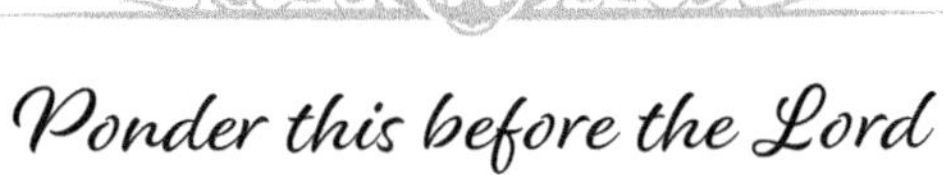

Ponder this before the Lord

Is Jesus calling you to "fail" as he "failed"? Is there a situation in your life that invites you to be a disappointment? Ask the Lord for courage and to remember who it is that you belong to and what your mission is.

9

Who's in Your Ninety-Eight?

So he told them this parable: "Which one of you, having a hundred sheep and losing one of them, does not leave the ninety-nine in the wilderness and go after the one that is lost until he finds it? When he has found it, he lays it on his shoulders and rejoices. And when he comes home, he calls together his friends and neighbors, saying to them, 'Rejoice with me, for I have found my sheep that was lost.' Just so, I tell you, there will be more joy in heaven over one sinner who repents than over ninety-nine righteous persons who need no repentance."

Luke 15:3-7

A beautiful, faithful, and quite extraordinary young woman I know writes to say that she's been feeling especially frustrated. She's trying so hard to lead a faithful life, she says. She attends daily Mass with such devotion—I've seen it. She has on multiple occasions traveled to serve the poorest of the poor in dire conditions for a month at a time, even leaving jobs and security behind to do so. She has endured substantial physical suffering and has had a number of serious operations. She offers every suffering, great and small, for the poor. Life is very good and blessed but hard, and she's grown a touch weary.

In prayer one day, she rests with the parable of the Good Shepherd. In her imagination she watches as the Good Shepherd leaves her, and so many others, to go after that one lost sheep. As he disappears into the hills in search of his lost one, she poses this question to him, "I'm trying so, so hard, Lord. You see how hard I am trying to lead a faithful, authentic Christian life. Why? Why did you leave me to go after the stray?"

And in her heart, she hears this reply: "Because I trust the other ninety-eight." Suddenly all of the other "sheep" around her take on the faces of so many other faithful friends and family, even saints and angels that accompany her unseen.

She writes to me to say, "Thank you for being one of my ninety-eight."

The Lord need never explain himself to you, but it seems to me he is very often willing to do so if we would ask with sincerity.

And most important of all, whether you are among the ninety-nine left behind in one another's company, or you are the one the shepherd has set out to find, we must take note with gratitude that our God is a God who searches for us until he finds us, then carries us home with joy—to rejoin the ninety-nine. It is not a burden to look for us when we are lost; it is his joy.

Though for today you may feel abandoned as the Shepherd goes in search of one who has gone astray, remember what a grace it is to be a part of the ninety-nine.

Ponder this before the Lord

Who is in your ninety-eight, your group of faithful, prayerful friends? Can you think of a time when you sensed the accompaniment of other believers around you or the angels and saints who helped you to remain faithful? Write a note or send a message to a few of your ninety-eight and thank them for accompanying you. Recommit yourself to accompanying them in return.

10

This Is the Way

Therefore the LORD waits to be gracious to you; therefore he will rise up to show mercy to you. For the LORD is a God of justice; blessed are all those who wait for him. Truly, O people in Zion, inhabitants of Jerusalem, you shall weep no more. He will surely be gracious to you at the sound of your cry; when he hears it, he will answer you. Though the Lord may give you the bread of adversity and the water of affliction, yet your Teacher will not hide himself any more, but your eyes shall see your Teacher. And when you turn to the right or when you turn to the left, your ears shall hear a word behind you, saying, "This is the way; walk in it."

Isaiah 30:18-21

My life as a writer has been very blessed. Writing about my faith has been some of the most meaningful work I've ever had, and I can hardly believe I get to do it sometimes.

But it's also challenging and can feel a little isolated. Your books are "out there somewhere" being read, or not. They rather disappear into the universe, and it's not all that often that you hear from someone who has actually read one of your books and found it helpful.

One day as I was headed into Adoration, I was grumbling about this in my heart. I'd just received a royalty check for about thirty-five dollars. My royalty checks have become a source of amusement to me and my husband (without whose support I could not be writing, by the way). I'm grateful he has a good sense of humor. But I've been writing too long not to know that there's not a big financial reward in it. The reward is elsewhere.

As I settled in for Adoration, I kneeled down and offered my heart up to the Lord. "Lord, it's very hard," I whispered. "I just wish I knew I was doing the right thing with my life and my skills. Maybe I should have gone to law school." I sat in the quiet with my head in my hands.

Just then a woman I did not know came in and sat down two rows in front of me and to the right. She got busy settling into prayer. Only a moment passed when—you guessed it—she pulled out a book I had written and started reading it. She paused now and then, underlining, making notes. And when she reached the end of the chapter, where I almost always offer a prompt for prayer, she took out her Bible and started praying with the prompt I had written.

And then I noticed this: as she set her Bible down and turned her face to the Lord in the Blessed Sacrament, she closed her eyes, and smiled. The warmest, most peaceful look came across her face and she sat that way for a long, long while.

Now, I have no way of knowing whether or not my little book helped her reach that beautiful place in prayer, but I am certain that the Lord was showing me in a very visceral way, "You are on a good path, and I am blessing it."

Ponder this before the Lord

Are you in a place of needing a little encouragement to know you are on a path that is taking you to the Lord, one that he is walking with you? It's alright to ask for a little confirmation or affirmation. Look for it first and foremost in God's word.

11

Very Unlike Beef

And do not grieve the Holy Spirit of God, with which you were marked with a seal for the day of redemption. Put away from you all bitterness and wrath and anger and wrangling and slander, together with all malice, and be kind to one another, tenderhearted, forgiving one another, as God in Christ has forgiven you.

Ephesians 4:30-32

People are so angry. Have you noticed? A driver rolls down his window and shouts poison at me, raises a fist, and hammers at his horn, all because I was driving the speed limit on a dangerous S curve in the rain. He wanted to speed. I walk into my vet to find a large sign on the check-in counter that reads: "Verbal or physical abuse will not be tolerated." Really? Apparently the women who run the front end of the clinic have been victim to this kind of thing on so many occasions that they had to post a warning sign about it. At the pool one day, a father who has brought his six young children screams at the lifeguard and gathers up his bewildered brood, marching them out in a fiery tirade because the lifeguard asked if his children could swim. Social media: sometimes, it just rages at you, doesn't it?

So much vitriol. And mostly not about the right things.

How did we all get so angry? So impatient? So put-upon that the slightest delay, inconvenience, or fumbling results in an eruption of overreaction? So filled with hate that random violence, school shootings, protests and unrest, even assassinations feel almost normal?

Maybe the answers to those questions don't matter as much as our response to the rage and ruin in the world. How are we called to reply?

Scripture is very clear. We are to be "the light of the world" and "salt of the earth" (Matthew 5:13-14). In short, we're called to be saints. G. K. Chesterton said it this way:

> The saint is a medicine because he is an antidote. Indeed that is why the saint is often a martyr; he is mistaken for a poison because he is an antidote. He will generally be found restoring the world to sanity by exaggerating whatever the world neglects. . . . He is not what the people want but rather what the people need. This is surely the very much mistaken meaning of those words to the first saints, "Ye are the salt of the earth." . . . Salt seasons and preserves beef, not because it is like beef; but because it is very unlike it.[2]

Just for today, let's exaggerate hope in the midst of hopelessness, and generosity in the midst of endless need. Let's smile at the guy who cuts us off in traffic and pray to his guardian angel to keep him safe. Let's make an extra effort to be kind in the face of the clerk who packed your bananas under the heavy cans of tomato sauce. Let's fast from every thought and starve out every desire to "get back at them." Let's repay unkindness and judgment with gentleness, mercy, and forgiveness. Let's be very unlike beef.

The world may laugh at you, or worse. It's okay. Let's exaggerate just like Jesus did.

Ponder this before the Lord

What is the world immediately around you neglecting? Can you respond as a light on a hill, putting away all wrangling, bitterness, and malice? Speak to the Lord about any resistance that comes up in your heart.

The Kneeling Mercy of Jesus

"Let the little children come to me, and do not stop them;
for it is to such as these that the kingdom of heaven belongs."
℘ Matthew 19:14 ℘

Our parish was hosting a Lenten "Day of Mercy," with confessions available from 12 to 9 pm. All day long, multiple visiting priests would tend to those in need of forgiveness. On that day, Eucharistic Adoration was moved into the main sanctuary, and so I held my Holy Hour there, praying amidst the souls visiting the stations for confession scattered throughout the church. It was a lovely grace to be in the presence of so many seeking the merciful face of God.

But this was my favorite moment.

A young family came in: several children, mom and dad. They filed neatly into a pew and all knelt down. Among them was a girl of about ten. She was clearly a bit distressed. Her mother and father leaned over her reassuringly, but she would not be comforted. At one point, the mother got up, left, and returned a few moments later with our parish priest—a lovely, thoughtful young man.

And he came, smiling—beaming really—and ever so gently knelt down in front of this little girl, his cassock spilling onto the ground. I was seated in such a way that, with the young girl's back to me, I could see our good shepherd make himself low so that he could look up into this precious child's face. Her shoulders were slouched and quivering. She was clearly frightened to go to confession. But this beautiful young priest smiled up at her with such authentic reassurance, even I was moved by the gesture half a church away.

They spoke for a moment, all the while our priest looking up at her, so kind and attentive. And then, after a moment of her own quiet prayer, she sheepishly approached a station, sat humbly face-to-face before a priest, and confessed her ten-year-old sins. Walking back to her pew to rejoin her family, the relief was palpable. She knelt and prayed once more with the kind of sweet earnestness only the forgiven possess.

The justice of the Almighty is indeed a fearsome thing, but his mercy kneels before us with tenderness and kindness everlasting; "His mercy endures forever" (Daniel 3:89). "Work out your own salvation with fear and trembling" (Philippians 2:12), and yet, "'Come,'" my heart says, 'seek his face!' Your face, LORD, do I seek. Do not hide your face from me" (Psalm 27:8-9). I thank the Lord for that priest, for his posture before that child—that she would seek the face of the Lord in the priest who heard her confession and offered her absolution. It might change the course of her life and all that she will contribute to the Church, and the world will be colored by it. Bless you, Father.

Ponder this before the Lord

Do you fear the Lord? Do you fear standing before him, owning your sin? Can you ask the Lord to give you a proper fear of offending him, all the while strengthening your faith in his mercy?

13

He is Mighty, Faithful, and Powerful

Who among the heavenly beings is like the Lord,
a God feared in the council of the holy ones,
great and awesome above all that are around him?
O Lord God of hosts,
who is as mighty as you, O Lord?
Your faithfulness surrounds you.
You rule the raging of the sea;
when its waves rise, you still them.
⊱Psalm 89:6-9⊰

I was in graduate school in Alaska and very far from family when I started having troubling symptoms. I saw a barrage of doctors and had multiple tests. Nothing was conclusive. One doctor said, "Maybe it's a tumor." Another told me I just needed a vacation.

Another tossed out a diagnosis of multiple sclerosis very casually, as though it were no big deal. I had an uncle who had lived much of his adult life in a wheelchair due to MS. I knew how hard it could be, what it cost him and his family. I was immediately catapulted into a dark and merciless future. I was so scared that I couldn't sleep or eat.

If I did anything right in that moment, it was this: I did not isolate and ruminate. Instead, I called the pastor at my church and left a message, explaining the situation and asking if I might speak to him. I knew how busy he was, and despite his full schedule, he called me back almost immediately, and I was struck by two things. One, the joy in his voice returning my call. And two, even more so by the *authority* in his voice.

This was a man who *knew* God's word, loved it, taught it brilliantly, made it come alive for his congregation. He gave me a perfect assignment. As I was about to launch into the horror that my future was sure to be—which, by the way, having lived with MS for thirty years I can definitively say, as hard as it's been, it's been graced too—he stopped me and said, "Whoa. Wait a minute. What do you know about the Lord?" He asked me to make a list: What did God's word say about him? It was a brilliant assignment. In minutes it rewrote my panic into trust, peace, and hope—a quaking hope, to be sure. I was still frightened, but I was also renewed in the knowledge of who God is.

By the time I hung up, I was reoriented. I had been staring at the problem and imagining the worst. But God's word told me he had a plan for me, for my flourishing—a future with hope, even if that was in a wheelchair. Even if that did mean a life of serious limitations. MS was not bigger than God. God is far, far greater than MS.

I have used this assignment countless times in my life when fear tempted me to doubt the God I know as almighty, forgiving, merciful, powerful, creative, tender, and so much more. God's word, my friends, is fear's kryptonite.

Ponder this before the Lord

Are you in an uncertain season, a time filled with fear of the future? Open your Bible and start collecting your favorite verses that describe God the Father, Jesus his Son, and the Holy Spirit. Rest with that list every night before bed. Repeat as needed. Add new names and attributes as God reveals them to you.

14

He Was There

Can a woman forget her nursing child,
or show no compassion for the child of her womb?
Even these may forget,
yet I will not forget you.
See, I have inscribed you on the palms of my hands.

Isaiah 49:15-16

She was as faithful a mother as any could be. She doted on her children, celebrated their victories, comforted them in their disappointments, encouraged them in their life choices. She was attentive and loving and gave up what would have been a smashing career in law in order to stay home and be available to her family. She had her children baptized, confirmed, and raised up in the faith she loved and that meant so much to her. Her husband even converted early in their marriage as a result of her holy and faithful example.

But, as sometimes happens, despite this mother's best and most sincere efforts, her only daughter fell away from her faith. The daughter struggled with depression and addiction, but to her credit got sober and began thriving in life and worked as a social worker advocating for the poor. When it came time for her to marry, however, she did not want to be married in the Church. Her mom was heartbroken, and somewhat baffled. She wondered, *What happened? What did I do wrong?*

Still, she helped her daughter prepare for the big day with love and generosity. She and her husband paid for the whole affair, as tradition would have it. She helped her daughter choose the dress, make plans, pick the menu, and prepare the table dressings, invitations, and seating charts. She embraced her new son-in-law as though he was her own child. She showed up, but all the while, inside her heart was aching at the lack of a sacramental ceremony.

On the day of the wedding, she was joyful and supportive and smiling in every photo. The day came off beautifully, but deep down inside, she still mourned. The next day as she awoke and was getting ready for her day, she stood over the sink, splashed water on her face and said, "Oh, Lord, I so wanted you to *be* there, to be invited."

In the quiet of her heart, she heard this clear reply, "But I was invited. I was there."

Suddenly the day alighted in her mind in a new way. Her daughter was a thoughtful and tender creature with an eye for those who suffered. She chose the caterer not because the food was the best but because they made a point to hire workers that other companies would not: former convicts, drugs addicts, and the like. When at the last minute a family member was unable to attend, the daughter chose to invite a young woman she knew didn't have many friends and was struggling to get sober.

Best of all, when it came time for the exchanging of vows, her daughter chose a very traditional verse from 1 Corinthians

13 but added her own twist, exchanging the word "love" for the name of her beloved. She read:

> Drew is patient; Drew is kind; Drew is not envious or boastful or arrogant or rude. Drew does not insist on his own way; he is not irritable or resentful. . . . Drew bears all things, believes all things, hopes all things, endures all things.

This mother stood there in front of the sink, her face still dripping from the water she had splashed on it now comingling with her tears, and heard the voice of the Lord once again in her heart: "I *was* invited. I was there."

Ponder this before the Lord

Has someone you love fallen away from their faith? Can you entrust them once again to his care, indeed to the very palm of his hand, and remember, God isn't finished with them just yet?

15

Ripples

Two are better than one, because they have a good
reward for their toil. For if they fall, one will lift up the
other; but woe to one who is alone and falls and does not
have another to help. Again, if two lie together, they keep
warm; but how can one keep warm alone? And though
one might prevail against another, two will withstand one.
A threefold cord is not quickly broken.
ℴEcclesiastes 4:9-12℞

It was a glorious, crisp Minnesota winter afternoon, and I
was out on the frozen lake walking my dogs. The snow
crunched beneath my heavy boots as my pups raced
and rolled and sniffed to their hearts' content. It is a favorite place to pray and to wonder about the majesty of God,
to get very small in the face of his grandeur.

My cell phone rang, and I dug it out of my winter coat pocket
and was greeted by the voice of a woman with a lovely southern
drawl, Jean. She struck me immediately. I could almost feel the
Holy Spirit coursing through satellites and cell towers to connect
us across such a distance. I remember at one point holding the
phone out in front of me and thinking, "*Who* is *this*?" Little did

I know this would be the beginning of a long-term and significant collaboration in pursuing the face of God.

Jean had taken an online prayer practicum with me. I began offering it online when Covid hit and we were no longer able to meet in person. She was calling because she runs an apostolate called Mary's Women of Joy in North Carolina, and they were interested in doing a study with me. I agreed, and I adapted my *Jesus Approaches* study for her group of about 200 women. For 12 weeks we met virtually, and I discovered 200 new faithful friends.

That study went so well that we did another based on *Love like a Saint*, and that led to two more in-person retreats and another study on Our Lady at Prayer. I'm scheduled to return to North Carolina for another retreat, and multiple chapters of Mary's Women of Joy have also taken the studies I first developed for Jean.

I count her as one of my most trusted prayer-warrior woman friends. And though we don't get to spend as much time together as we might like, we are in each other's lives now—a connection that only the Holy Spirit could have created.

It's one of his favorite things to do: to tether us to one another, to the Sacred Heart of Jesus, to the heart of the Father. It's what he does. And very often, these connections have a ripple effect, like a pebble in a pond, spreading out in endless concentric circles of connection and resonance.

Ponder this before the Lord

Recall a time when a connection you made in your life was clearly a gift from God. What happened? How were you and others blessed? Give thanks to the Lord for this ripple of grace.

16

Bit by Bit

Then the one who had received the five talents came forward, bringing five more talents, saying, "Master, you handed over to me five talents; see, I have made five more talents." His master said to him, "Well done, good and trustworthy slave; you have been trustworthy in a few things, I will put you in charge of many things; enter into the joy of your master."

⅋Matthew 25:20-21⅌

One of my favorite summers was spent working on a horse farm. I'd grown up with horses and I loved being at the barn and working with these beautiful beasts. I also got to work the polo matches by helping tack the ponies, cooling them down after a chukker, and cleaning tack. It was delightful work for me. And I learned a surprising amount. It was there I met Paul.

Paul was a professional polo player. He had traveled the world playing against kings and princes and sheiks. He was small, wiry, and brutally strong. His forearms were reminiscent of Popeye. He could easily "pony-up" with six horses: that is, he would ride one horse and lead six other horses, three on his right and three on his left, holding all six lead ropes with one hand, while galloping for thirty-minute sets around the polo field.

But it was his training of the young horses that really stuck with me. When he identified a new colt or filly that seemed a good fit for polo, one of the first things he did was to hang dozens of polo mallets from the ceiling of a stall. They hung in such a way that when the colt entered the stall, the mallets would lightly bump into him from about the shoulders up, gently clacking and smacking against one another and the colt any time he moved. Paul would put the colt's oats—a delectable treat that was hard for a horse to resist—in a trough in the middle of the mallets. So if the colt wanted his oats, he had to endure a little clacking and bumping and banging of mallets.

First the colt would be in there for an hour, skittish and uncomfortable about all this banging and strangeness, leery of these odd sticks in his stall, but eventually the smell of the grain would win out and the colt would risk it. He'd allow the bumping and banging and gobble up his oats in a quick minute and then retreat to the edge of the stall where he could avoid the mallets.

Gradually, Paul would work the colt's stall time up to two hours and then several and before you knew it, the colt would saunter into the stall as though it were the most normal thing in the world to have mallets hanging from the ceiling, swinging past his head, bumping into his haunches and all the rest. It was a brilliant teaching tool.

Of course, if Paul had simply tacked the colt and taken him into a polo match without this prior training, the colt would have been traumatized by all of the mallets swinging and clacking and cracking the ball. The colt would have been ruined for the sport. The law of gradualism built the colt's confidence and comfort.

How often does God use a similar tactic on me, allowing me to grow into my work, slowly, gradually, bit by bit, strengthening me with smaller tests to prepare for the greater test ahead?

Ponder this before the Lord

Are there "mallets" hanging from your ceiling? Can you see how the Lord is gradually preparing you for greater work ahead? Can you trust in his method? Speak to him about your fears and anxieties.

17

Manna from Dairy Queen

For their hunger you gave them bread from heaven, and
for their thirst you brought water for them out of the rock.
Nehemiah 9:15

Following a double mastectomy, we were really hopeful that no more treatment would be required for breast cancer. But after they sent my tumors off for more examination, it was determined that chemotherapy would greatly reduce my risk of recurrence. Reluctantly and with some serious dread, I called and made an appointment with the oncologist to discuss my options.

I was quite literally hanging up the phone from that rather ominous call when my husband walked in the door and announced, "I just got laid off."

You can't make up moments like this.

We put our heads down and prayed and continued to trust that the Lord was working this all for good. My husband sent out resumes and I worked to reschedule retreats and talks, even leading a pilgrimage to Italy, as I was unsure if I'd be well enough to do this work. We prepared as best we could for months of chemotherapy.

As unlikely as it sounds, my husband getting laid off turned out to be a tremendous gift. It meant he would be free to help take care of me as I began treatment, which wasn't easy. Additionally, he was laid off from a job he found completely frustrating. He would often return home from that job in a kind of morose cloud. Even as we worried about having no income, it was a relief to both of us that he was free of that stress.

But it gets even better.

After several months of my husband sending out resumes and interviewing, and as my energy waned more and more—some days it was all I could do to walk from my bed to the bathroom—my husband received a job offer. It was a good offer for a better job with better pay and benefits. He would begin this new work the same week I had my last chemotherapy infusion—which meant he would be gone all day when I would be the sickest and weakest I had been thus far.

Without even a moment's hesitation, two of my sisters made plans to drop everything going on in their own homes to come and take care of me so my husband could start his new job. One sister came and tended to me for more than a week, and when she had to leave, the other made arrangements to arrive the same afternoon. They made meals, did laundry, walked the dogs, changed my bedsheets when I was too weak to do so, and waited on my every need with cheerful tenderness, including a few trips to the local Dairy Queen for vanilla shakes as it was the only food I could tolerate.

And this was on top of so many friends who stepped up with prayers, cards, and gifts of every sort. It was a huge relief to my husband to know I was so well cared for, and he was able to start a new job with far less worry about my bald head.

God is never up in heaven slapping his forehead, looking down on our trials and suffering, saying, "Sorry, kid, I never saw that coming. Good luck."

And while this was far from an easy season of life, it was incredibly fruitful in demonstrating the Lord's provision again and again and again.

Ponder this before the Lord

Recall a time when the Lord surprised you with provision. What happened? What did you learn? Give thanks to him and renew your faith and trust in his good plans for you.

Allowed to Grow

Grow in the grace and knowledge of
our Lord and Savior Jesus Christ.
2 Peter 3:18

A publisher had asked me to write a book on the Rosary. I would offer a thorough history of its development, a little Mariology for those who did not understand the role of Mary in prayer and the life of the Church, and then meditations on each of the mysteries. At that stage, there were only fifteen mysteries, moments in the life of Jesus and Mary that served as points of reflection and meditation, such as the birth of Jesus and finding Jesus in the Temple, the scourging of Jesus, and his resurrection and ascension. I set to work with great joy and enthusiasm.

I was young and fervent. It was my first book, and I confess there were a few moments in it that were a touch stringent. Nothing terrible, but in looking back I might have softened a phrase here and there for those who were new to the faith, struggling to pray, or struggling to believe in God's mercy. After the book was released, when I saw those two spots in it, the strident tone made me cringe.

But our God is a God of endless chances to make things right.

A few years after my first version of the book was released, Pope John Paul II added five new reflections called the Luminous Mysteries. These focused on Jesus at his baptism, the wedding feast of Cana, his teaching of the coming of his father's kingdom, the transfiguration, and the Last Supper as the institution of the Eucharist. It was decided that my first book would be pulled so that I could add a chapter of reflections on these newly added mysteries. Then the book would be rereleased under a new title.

My publisher sent me the entire book back for editing—which meant I got to go back to those spots that came across as too harsh to my older and wiser ear, and soften them. It nearly brought me to tears to think of how generous the Lord was in giving me this opportunity for revision—in my book and in my heart.

It was Peter, our rock, the man appointed to lead that tender, young Church, and who had earlier betrayed the Lord three times—and in such a public way—who knew this God of endless second chances. Despite his failure, Peter was recommissioned after the resurrection. The Lord even put him in charge of the whole community of new believers. Think of that responsibility. He must have been overwhelmed at the Lord's mercy. And he was allowed to grow and learn.

Peter knew—and he reminds us in his letters—that we are to continually grow in our understanding, continually cultivate virtue, and continually chase after holiness. It's not a one-and-done proposition but an ongoing life posture. Let's embrace this reminder together to keep growing.

I may want instant perfection, but the Lord is so much more humane than that. I thank him for his generosity and gentleness in working with humanity, in allowing us to grow slowly, sometimes weakly, sometimes failing and falling back. Always ready to give us another chance.

Ponder this before the Lord

Is there something you would rewrite in your life, great or small? Can you bring this to the Lord and ask for his mercy and grace to continue to grow in holiness?

19

His Intention or Mine?

I am God, and there is no other;
I am God, and there is no one like me,
declaring the end from the beginning
and from ancient times things not yet done,
saying, "My purpose shall stand,
and I will fulfill my intention," . . .
I have spoken, and I will bring it to pass;
I have planned, and I will do it.
Isaiah 46:9-11

I'd been working on it for months, filling a notebook with work ideas for the very book you hold in your hands. I always begin any new work writing it out by hand. Handwriting engages far more of your brain than typing. It's rare I go anywhere without a fresh pen and notebook, especially when I'm working on a book.

About this time, my husband and I took a short vacation to visit my sister over the Triduum and Easter. We relished attending all the Holy Week services as visitors in her parish. On Easter Monday, we packed our bags and headed home. During our return flight, I pulled out my notebook and worked a bit, reflecting on the graces of this holy season. Then I tucked my notebook—with so many months of work inside—into the seatback pocket.

And left it there. Exited the plane without it. Didn't even realize I'd left it until we got home and I started unpacking. I have never forgotten a notebook like that before. Never. My spiritual director said, "I think God is up to something in this." She was smiling.

What ensued was several weeks' worth of back and forth with the airline, describing my notebook in detail, giving them my seat assignment so they'd know exactly where I left it. I even identified the various colors of ink I'd used on its pages.

One week passed, then another, and then another. By then, I'd started a new notebook and prayed every day, "Lord, please return my notebook to me. You know how much work is in it. But not my will but yours be done."

Finally after several months, I got a definitive note from the airline: "We looked for your lost item but despite our best efforts were unable to locate it. We now consider your case closed." Left with no other recourse, I went back to work in earnest.

Despite this setback, the book seemed intent on writing itself. It rather spilled onto the page; I even managed a few extra entries, just in case. And that doesn't usually happen for me. Day by day, as I worked closer and closer to the deadline for the manuscript, the whole experience became a vivid reminder that it is the Lord who appoints our days, our work, our mission. None of us is deserving or worthy. None of us conjures graces for ourselves; they are always bestowed by the Father. None of us is capable of producing excellent work, like the excellent wine at the wedding feast at Cana, without the touch of the Holy Spirit.

God has plenty of ideas, energy, and creativity. The Father is replete with resources, graces, mercy, and love. There is no lack in him. And though notebooks may go missing, no work that he has begun will lie fallow and unfinished. His purpose—in you—shall stand.

Ponder this before the Lord

Resting in this passage from Isaiah, recall a moment when the Lord seemed to fulfill a promise despite setbacks. What happened, and what did you learn about the Father and about yourself?

20

Even for Just One

I pray that you may have the power to comprehend, with all the saints, what is the breadth and length and height and depth, and to know the love of Christ that surpasses knowledge, so that you may be filled with all the fullness of God.

Ephesians 3:18-19

It was my first trip to Australia—my very first gig in another hemisphere, a women's day retreat. It was the first in a series of events I'd be leading over the next three weeks, and I was beyond excited. The hall would hold about seventy-five, and there was a bit of worry that we might have to turn women away, but we entrusted the event to the Holy Spirit and prepared to receive those who attended.

The morning of the event, as I walked into the hall, I could sense the host was avoiding me. I scanned the room. There were no more than half a dozen women scattered across far too many seats. We'd ordered far too much food, far too many books, and far too many programs. As my first event in the country, I was worried about what the next three weeks would bring.

I've been at this work too long not to know that sometimes, nobody shows. A spiritual director once told me, "Do not despise small beginnings," and then he'd remind me that the young church began with only a handful. My husband is also very good at reminding me to speak as though the venue is standing room only and give it the very best I've got, no matter the number of people before me. And that day, I did just that. The day came off well despite the small numbers.

But something very curious did happen. There was one woman who arrived a little late. She sneaked in quietly, sat toward the back—and hung on every word I said. She left before I could greet her, but then I noticed that same woman at my talk the next night, and the next, and every night I was speaking around Sydney for the next several weeks. She came to every single one of my talks in that area and listened as though her life depended on it.

I never did meet her, but I have sometimes wondered if my whole trip halfway around the globe was simply for her. Because that's exactly how much the Lord loves us and the lengths he will go to meet us, touch us, heal us. Even for the sake of just one.

Even for the sake of you.

Ponder this before the Lord

Try to imagine how much the Lord loves you. How deep is his love, how wide, how all-consuming? Is his love for you a river, an ocean, a universe? Through the intercession of St. Paul, ask the Lord to give you a visual image of his love for you and then, receive it.

21

Flawless in His Eyes

You are altogether beautiful, my love;
and there is no flaw in you.
Song of Songs 4:7

The day I got my head shaved, the heat index in Minnesota was 108 degrees. As I sat in the chair at the salon, a stylist who donated her time to women going through chemo asked me, "So, what do you want to do here?"

I told her, "Shave it, shave it off."

She drew her fingers through my hair that remained; there was still quite a lot of it. It was long and wavy and, where it still held on, quite thick. But I was losing it in big, painful clumps, more and more day by day. It was time to be finished with it.

She hesitated. "You don't want to just cut it shorter?"

I shook my head, "No, take it all off, please. It's hot and itchy, and it hurts."

I was one of those rare chemo patients who, when my hair was falling out, my head became extremely tender. It hurt especially when laying on the pillow at night. Better to get it over with and shave my head bald. She pulled out the clippers.

But here's the thing: I loved being bald. My whole life I've had a head of thick, heavy, long hair. To make it look nice took some effort and time. Taking a shower always involved two towels, one for my body and one for my hair. My hair had eaten up gallons upon gallons of shampoo and conditioner and various hair products for more than fifty years. It had become crazy expensive to get it cut or colored. It clogged drains and made a mess. It was lovely, but it was also exhausting.

Being bald was delightfully easy. Such a timesaver. So cool and breezy. I took to it immediately.

I taunted my husband, who has shaved his own head bald for decades, "You never told me how easy this was!" We took playful pictures of the back of our heads together with a caption, "Who wears it best?" I think I won that bet.

I would never say, "Cancer is delightful!" But I will say, God never stops surprising me, even in cancer—and especially in suffering. That we could find blessing, even outright joy and laughter in it, is evidence of God's grace and tenderness. It further heightened my awareness of the tenderness and love of my husband, who would sooner chew off his own arm than ever make me feel anything less than completely desirable and beautiful in his eyes.

Ponder this before the Lord

How does the Lord see you? Is there someone in your life who looks on you with such love and tenderness that you can feel the Lord looking at you through their eyes? Do you look at someone that way? What does this teach you about the Father's love for you?

22

A Surprising Package

I am a rose of Sharon,
a lily of the valleys.
◈Song of Songs 2:1◈

I was in Adoration when my older brother left a message asking me to call him back as soon as I could. When he answered the phone he said, "I just had this feeling I was supposed to call you first." The news? He and his wife had just discovered that their baby, number ten, almost certainly would be born with Down syndrome.

He sounded anxious, uncertain, and he said his wife was taking it really hard. I tried to reassure him. I knew quite a number of families and had close friends who had children with Down syndrome. It wasn't easy, but every one of them would say that their child with Downs was the greatest gift God had ever given them. I remember one woman telling me, "It's like having an angel living in your house." Another told me, "My boy with Downs taught me how to love."

Still there was a great deal of uncertainty. Not only in the short term—hearing and heart health and other vulnerabilities that often come with the diagnosis—but in the long term. Who would care for her after my brother and his wife were gone? Naturally, they were awash in worry and wondering about the future. But their faith was strong. They put their trust in God and in the plan he had for this little vulnerable life, and prepared for the baby's arrival.

Margaret Rose, "Rosebud," "The Bud," was born in all other respects healthy and well, just in need of a little oxygen for several weeks. She immediately captured the hearts of her entire household. Her older sisters and brothers could barely let two seconds pass without kissing her or cuddling with her. Pictures from the hospital showed my brother and sister-in-law with broad, peaceful smiles and arms tucked around their precious new bundle. At a recent wedding I observed as aunts, uncles, brothers, sisters, and cousins all fought over who got to hold her.

It was a few months before I was able to meet her in person. My sister-in-law and I sat in her living room as she breastfed Maggie Rose.

"I wish I could take back all of that initial fear that I had," my sister-in-law said. She beamed at her newborn and stroked her hair.

She went on, "If the Lord walked in the room right now and said, 'I will take back that extra chromosome right now if you wish it,' I'd say, 'Oh no, Lord, don't!' Maggie is exactly who she is supposed to be and I wouldn't want to change one single thing about her." "The Bud" continues to thrive. Her smile is like a little strike of happy lightning, the purest, most potent shock of innocence and delight.

How often God's greatest gifts come in the most surprising packages: the illness that teaches us compassion and patience, the deprivation that strengthens our perseverance, the loss that turns out to be gain, the little child with an extra chromosome who fills your heart with so much joy and love, you feel it might burst.

Ponder this before the Lord

When has the Lord surprised you with an unlikely gift? Can you think of a time when you had a dramatic change of heart once you turned to the Lord in faith, trusting in his goodness? What happened, and what did you learn?

23

"Because Sometimes"

But now thus says the Lord,
he who created you, O Jacob,
he who formed you, O Israel:
Do not fear, for I have redeemed you;
I have called you by name, you are mine.
When you pass through the waters, I will be with you;
and through the rivers, they shall not overwhelm you;
when you walk through fire you shall not be burned,
and the flame shall not consume you.
For I am the Lord your God,
the Holy One of Israel, your Savior.
Isaiah 43:1-3

I first met Pat when I was leading a prayer group online. She was bright, creative, a deep well, and truly alive in her prayer. Over sixteen weeks, I got to know her heart quite well.

It was later that I got to know her as a two-time cancer survivor.

Not long after I was diagnosed with breast cancer for the second time, and as I was awaiting the start of chemotherapy following surgery, a large box arrived from Pat. It was filled to the brim with aids to help me through chemotherapy. Attached to each item was a yellow sticky with a handwritten note indicating its purpose. It was a thorough cache, and I lined up each item on a long shelf in my bathroom and took pictures of my little army of soldiers of comfort to send to all my friends. "My arsenal!" read the caption.

Among the ranks stood:

Fragrance-free moisturizer: "Because sometimes during chemo scents can make you nauseated."

Stomach settling lozenges: "Because sometimes you need something to soothe your tummy."

Vanilla yogurt-covered raisins: "Because sometimes you need a little snack while at chemo. This was my favorite."

Hydration packets in a variety of flavors: "Because sometimes during chemo water tastes funny and you need to stay hydrated."

Dry mouth lozenges: "Because sometimes chemo can make your mouth really dry."

Lip ointment: "Because sometimes chemo can cause mouth sores."

On and on it went; like a clown car of chemo tonics, they just kept coming out of the box.

Not only was her gift incredibly useful, more than that it was a tonic to my nerves. Here was someone who had been down this road before—twice!—who generously shared resources and her own experience so that I wouldn't have to walk into it in the dark. I felt so much better prepared for treatment and far less isolated and fearful. I would walk into this fire, yes, but I had a renewed faith that it would not consume me because I was not alone.

God's word does not promise a life free of fire, flood, or terror, but he does promise to be with us in those trials. Sometimes the way he chooses to accompany us is through our friends. It was Pat that sent me that box of chemo tricks and tonics, but it was Jesus, too.

The best part was still to come. As I was finishing up my treatment, my brother-in-law also received a serious cancer diagnosis. He would require chemotherapy, too. And the next time I saw him I came prepared with a big box of chemo tricks and tonics, each with a note, just in case.

Ponder this before the Lord

How have you experienced the Lord's accompaniment through some suffering or trial? How did he reveal himself to you through another? Write that person a note and thank them for their fidelity to you and to the Lord.

24

Faithful, Not Famous

On the last day of the festival, the great day, while Jesus
was standing there, he cried out, "Let anyone who is
thirsty come to me, and let the one who believes in me
drink. As the scripture has said, 'Out of the believer's
heart shall flow rivers of living water.'"
John 7:37-38

I moved my column over to Substack, I realized, about
three years too late. By the time I embraced this plat-
form, it was so saturated with other writers, some quite
fine, and all competing so fiercely for readers, that I knew I
had missed the boat. Even the smallest amount I could ask
for a subscription was expensive. There weren't options to
ask for less.

So much for my grand scheme to create a new revenue stream.

Social media and the internet have always been a bane to me.
When I first started writing, all you needed to do was to write
the finest book that you could. The marketing, advertising, and
promotion was done by an in-house team. I just had to show up
for interviews and book fairs and the like.

Thirty years later, every publishing house in the world has shifted course. They all want to know from their authors, "How will YOU promote your work?" It's a fair question, but not one I'm very comfortable answering. I find social media exhausting and mostly banal. The idea of sitting down to promote my book, especially through those means, literally makes me nauseated. It's just not for me.

Don't get me wrong, sales is a truly sacred task. I want my books to find the readers who really need them. And to get my books into the hands of those who would benefit from them takes some thoughtfulness. I'm grateful to those who do exactly that work.

Still, Jesus never had a marketing team. He *walked* through Galilee, healing, teaching, and preaching. Think of that cadence, walking. How would your day change if you thought about walking through it, rather than racing at the speed of a supercomputer?

With the exception of a short jaunt as an infant into exile in Egypt, Jesus never even left his own country. He didn't have a scheme for worldwide promotions. He never posted on social media. There are no snapshots of Jesus hanging out at the Sea of Galilee with his "bros." Think #theTwelve. He left his entire hard-won enterprise in the hands of a few rather frightened apostles with zero acumen for sales.

Jesus does not call me to be famous or fast; he doesn't even call me to be successful. He calls me to be faithful. Certainly, Jesus can make himself present and known through the bombardment of social media, just as surely as he kept company with tax collectors and prostitutes. But let's be really careful to drop the slightest concern over the numbers of likes, followers, or even dollars in our bank accounts. Let's resist the temptation to deliver something quickly rather than thoughtfully and led by the Holy Spirit. Let's concentrate on being faithful to the Lord and present to those he places on our path, and to walking with them, slowly and surely. Let's feed his sheep, not count them.

Ponder this before the Lord

Are you feeling distracted by social media or the trappings of technology? Rest with the verses above and ask the Lord to establish your cadence with him. Ask him to give you a fresh infilling of the Holy Spirit, that from your heart, his living water will flow—first to slake your own thirst for him, and then to help temper the thirst of the world around you.

25

Who's in Your Bouquet?

Let my beloved come to his garden,
and eat its choicest fruits.
℘Song of Songs 4:16℆

It was easy to pray with this passage from Song of Songs—this moment when the Bride invites her Beloved to "come to his garden," the one she had been preparing for him.

This was the image that flooded my prayer. I pictured a huge flower garden—a touch overgrown, but mature, robust, filled with every kind of blossom imaginable. Jesus and I walked from flower to flower admiring this mature, blooming garden, a thriving meadow that we had grown together. He would stop and hover over the biggest blooms, smelling their aroma and admiring their color and beauty. Then I'd say, "Oh, but Lord, look at *this* one!" And we'd move on to the next.

At some point I turned to him and said, "Please, won't you pick a bouquet for your mom?" He flashed a broad, beaming smile and then quickly flew around the garden choosing the most beautiful blossoms of all, a wide variety of color and fragrance and bloom, and carefully gathered up each selection in a huge bouquet.

But after a moment, he leaned over a rose bush, and with gentleness and reverence he plucked the most beautiful white rose I have ever seen. In my heart, I knew that rose was my friend "Bella." She was a younger woman that I had mentored in one way or another over the years. She sent me a lovely note at one point along the journey of our friendship and thanked me for teaching her how to pray with Scripture. She went on to receive certification in spiritual direction. She serves brilliantly in her parish and witnesses to her whole family, especially her children, even taking one young son on a pilgrimage to attend the canonization of Sts. Carlo Acutis and Pier Giorgio Frassati. She is a remarkable soul, and I could see from the first moment that we met that the Lord had special plans for her.

Jesus looked down on this "rose" with the most profound affection. And all I could think of was how I couldn't wait to tell my friend that she was in a bouquet the Lord had handpicked especially for his holy Mother.

We don't always know the seeds we are planting or how beautifully they might one day bloom, and how delightful this must be to Jesus—or his momma.

Ponder this before the Lord

Can you trust that even though you may not see the ripened fruit or the full blossoming flower, the Lord sees, and he knows the plans he has for every seed you have ever planted? Yes, Jesus is at work in the garden of you, and you might one day be surprised and delighted by the fruit he is helping you to produce.

26

Into Hiding

O my dove, in the clefts of the rock,
in the covert of the cliff,
let me see your face,
let me hear your voice;
for your voice is sweet,
and your face is lovely.
∐Song of Songs 2:14∎

When I was returning to the Church in my late twenties, I discovered perpetual Adoration. Frequently, after I finished work very late, I would visit an Adoration chapel open all night. In those precious hours of quiet and hiding, on my knees before the Lord in the Blessed Sacrament, I discovered the Rosary of the Holy Wounds. (See the appendix.)

This rosary was given to Sr. Mary Martha Chambon (1841–1907) of the Monastery of the Visitation of Chambery. Just as St. Faustina was given the Chaplet of Divine Mercy, so Sr. Mary Martha received this rosary along with the long list of promises that are offered to those who pray it. They include: "My wounds will repair yours," "Plunge your actions into my wounds, and they will be of value," "When you have trouble, something to suffer, quickly place it in my wounds and the pain will be alleviated." This simple entreaty for healing of the soul quickly became one of my favorite devotions. I have prayed it daily since.

I often teach this rosary to groups when I travel to speak, and without fail, people are drawn to it—or rather, drawn into it. After one retreat, however, a woman approached me and asked, "But how do you do that? How do you place your wounds into the wounds of Christ?" I stammered in my reply. I had a sense of what that meant to me, but it was so personal, so deep, that there really weren't words to explain it.

I found a far more thoughtful response in a compendium of Carthusian devotions to the Sacred Heart. To "read the wounds of Christ," that is, to understand them more fully, these holy monks drew upon the vivid themes of the Canticles: "The Holy Spirit says to us in the Canticle, 'Come, O, my dove, into the clefts of the rock.'"[3] They equated this hiding place with the Holy Wounds of Jesus.

One monk recommends:

The soul should fly away as a timid dove, and take refuge in the clefts of the Rock, namely in the Wounds of Jesus Christ, and above all in the deep hollow place . . . in the Wound of the Side of Jesus and in His Heart. There she has nothing more to dread. If she builds her nest in the Heart of Jesus, if she there deposits her good works, there finds shelter, there rests and takes her sleep, the evil spirits will never attempt to set their snares for her; they dare not approach the Wounds and the Heart of Jesus.[4]

How I long to hide in the heart of Jesus, where no evil dares to enter.

Ponder this before the Lord

What wound would you hide in the cleft of the rock of his Sacred Heart? An illness, a betrayal, a disappointment? Can you borrow this ancient wisdom, purified and fashioned through lives of asceticism, and take refuge in the Sacred Heart of Jesus? What would that mean for you?

27

Restoration

Return to your stronghold, O prisoners of hope;
today I declare that I will restore to you double.
෨Zechariah 9:12ଔ

I was visiting a friend in Los Angeles. He was a professional musician and toured with some famous artists throughout his career, including "Reg." Reg was a successful guitarist and composer and a very faithful Christian. When he wasn't touring, he would serve as a musician at his church. While in LA, I was invited to a rehearsal Reg was having for an upcoming worship concert sponsored by his church.

I tucked myself into the back of the auditorium as Reg and his band began tuning their instruments in preparation for rehearsal. Reg fiddled with his guitar, over and over, strumming and tuning, his fingers, light and agile, running various riffs. Even while simply warming up, his talent was apparent as was his joy in playing.

He'd stop every once in a while and look at his guitar with something like awe, a twinkle in his eye. It was curious. I'm a musician myself and I know that musicians develop very strong relationships with their instruments, but something else was at play here.

Smiling, he told the story.

Several weeks prior, his favorite guitar, the one he wrote all of his hit songs on, the one he'd had forever, the one that felt like a part of his own body because he'd played on it so long, was stolen. He went into serious mourning. What would he do? It was irreplaceable. How could this have happened? He struggled to pray for the person who stole it. But eventually, his Christian heart won out, he accepted that the guitar was gone, prayed for the thief, thanked God for his many blessings, and went guitar shopping.

That day, as he fiddled with his new guitar, he beamed. He told his band, "And wouldn't you know it, God gave me a new guitar that I like even better!"

This is a principle living within the very heart of God—he desires nothing less for his people than total restoration. And not just restoration, but restoration that surpasses the old—restoration that is magnified, improved, even better.

Of course, some losses are far more difficult than a guitar. We might feel robbed of any number of things—dignified work, security, relationships. In the face of loss, let's cling to the knowledge that our God is a God of restoration, and let's never lose sight of his power to repair and even improve our circumstances.

Ponder this before the Lord

Have you lost something important, something you loved? A home, a friend, a job, maybe even a marriage? Or has something been taken from you? Your health, security, your hope? Pray for the grace to believe that the Lord has something even better in store for you.

28

Take Your Turn

O afflicted one, storm-tossed, and not comforted,
I am about to set your stones in antimony,
and lay your foundations with sapphires,
I will make your pinnacles of rubies,
your gates of jewels,
and all your wall of precious stones.
All your children shall be taught by the LORD,
and great shall be the prosperity of your children.
In righteousness you shall be established;
you shall be far from oppression, for you shall not fear;
and from terror, for it shall not come near you.
›Isaiah 54:11-14‹

A dear friend, after nearly forty years of marriage in which she raised six children, two with challenging disabilities, and after caring now for more than a dozen grandchildren over the past decade—and all this after having given up a career in teaching so she could stay home and tend her own—has realized, with some trepidation, that she may need a little healing.

She starts slowly, speaking with a spiritual director, her priest, and friends she trusts. Soon she adds onto her healing regimen a therapist, and after some time, she takes the very bold step to go on an intensive week-long healing retreat that promises some serious breakthroughs. Like a heart transplant that saves your life—replacing a broken heart for a new, functioning, healthy heart—one still has to have their chest opened up, vulnerable and exposed. The old heart must be removed—leaving you literally heartless for a moment, if it wasn't for the heart-lung machine—before that new heart can make its home in you. Healing, whether emotional or spiritual or both, is a bumpy, unpredictable thing with high tides, crashing storms, and low quiet moments that mean wading through years of lies, distress, and fear until finally you can rest in the peace of truth.

But this is her path, and for whatever reason, this is the time that the Lord has set aside for her own healing work. She moves toward it with extraordinary courage.

And this teaches me: we're never too old to heal. It's never too late to do our emotional work, our spiritual work. Perhaps we didn't process painful events when we were young because we were just trying to survive something difficult or dangerous. Maybe we've been so busy taking care of other people that we haven't made time to take care of our own needs. Maybe the idea of broaching past wounds is simply too exhausting or terrifying. Easier to stick your head in the sand or have another drink or distract yourself with a million nonessential things.

But it is not too late. What's more, the Lord sees you, just as you are, and he knows your wounds and needs for healing better than you do. Your need for healing is no surprise to him—it doesn't worry him or intimidate him. And he is a tender, gentle, respectful healer. He won't force healing on any of us, but he will offer it at any moment we need it.

Is it your time? Time to take your turn into healing? It's never too late.

Ponder this before the Lord

Have you settled? Resigned yourself to some chronic pain because you cannot imagine the Lord is interested in healing you and making you whole—in giving you a new, strong, beautiful, fleshy heart? Ask him about this and what it will take for you to take one step toward healing.

29

Into the Deep

Once while Jesus was standing beside the lake of Gennesaret, and the crowd was pressing in on him to hear the word of God, he saw two boats there at the shore of the lake; the fishermen had gone out of them and were washing their nets. He got into one of the boats, the one belonging to Simon, and asked him to put out a little way from the shore. Then he sat down and taught the crowds from the boat. When he had finished speaking, he said to Simon, "Put out into the deep water and let down your nets for a catch." Simon answered, "Master, we have worked all night long but have caught nothing. Yet if you say so, I will let down the nets." When they had done this, they caught so many fish that their nets were beginning to break.

ଔLuke 5:1-6ଔ

It was an exceptional season of life and work. As I was recovering from cancer, I received an invitation to take on some of the most important work of my life. My reach and responsibilities were expanding in fresh and unexpected ways. Jesus was asking me spiritually and professionally to put out into the deep, and it was dark and frightening out there—a long, long way from the safety of shore.

I didn't feel up to the task. A long list of reasons amassed in my head: I wasn't smart enough, well-educated enough, creative enough. I wasn't enough. And just like Simon, I was trying to talk Jesus out of his invitation. "But Lord, I'm not ready for the deep." "But Lord, I'm not worthy of the deep." "But Lord, I've tried on my own and it's gone nowhere." "But Lord . . ."

Then I noticed something I had never seen in that passage before: Jesus was in the boat. He didn't send Simon off alone into the dark; he stayed in the boat. He was right there with Simon, in his boat. They put out into the deep together.

And he's in my boat, too. And he's not going to abandon me. If he is expanding the reach or responsibility of my work, just like he was preparing Simon to do, even though I may have failed on my own initiative in the past, and even if I was exhausted with trying for naught, I put out into the deep knowing that Jesus is in my boat and he will not abandon me. He's with me—in the deep.

He's with you, too.

Ponder this before the Lord

Is Jesus asking you to do something that seems doomed to fail? Something illogical or unlikely? Is he stretching you beyond your own skill or comfort zone? What is that invitation, and how are you responding? Speak to Jesus about these things.

30

Believe

In the beginning was the Word, and the Word was with God, and the Word was God. He was in the beginning with God. All things came into being through him, and without him not one thing came into being. What has come into being in him was life, and the life was the light of all people. The light shines in the darkness, and the darkness did not overcome it.

ɛɔJohn 1:1-5ɔɘ

It was such an ordinary day when her phone rang. My dear friend, a devout Christian woman who was one of the first people to teach me how to pray with God's word, answered it. A man's voice met her, saying, "Ma'am, I'm a homicide detective. I'm afraid I have some very bad news."

She listened in quiet shock to hear that her only son had been murdered by a homeless drug addict on the street in another state. Police caught the perpetrator and he was in jail awaiting charges. I learned of this horror through a text message. My friend, so bereft, could not even speak the words into existence by her own tongue. Still, she wanted me to know because she knew I would pray, my parents would pray, my friends would pray, and maybe together, we could help her to carry this unimaginable burden.

This is not the world I imagined I would grow old in. Nevertheless, here we are.

I wish I could say that this was the only person I knew who had been touched by this crime as old as Cain and Abel, but sadly I know a few people who have lost loved ones to murder. How in the world do you carry that? What do you do with such terrors of the night? And how dare I say, "Be encouraged!" in light of such malevolence? When we find ourselves confronted by serious evil, where can we turn?

To the cross.

We must turn to the cross. We must fall at the foot of the cross and cling to it with all our might and know that the shadow the cross casts over the world is long and dark and terrifying to the evil spirits that prowl about the world. The cross, upon which Jesus suffered so horrifically and died, abandoned by most of his closest friends. The cross that he anticipated and accepted in obedience and dread. That bitter wood thrust into the earth by wicked hands and evil hearts and probably a myriad of indifferent souls just following orders because that's what they were told to do.

The cross. Bring your deepest, darkest pain and suffering to the foot of the cross and moan and wail as you will along with the Lord. He is not indifferent to your pain, but he carries it, reverences it, enters into it, and—just like his own suffering—he can transform it into something powerful and effective for good.

Go to the cross. Bring it all to the cross.

But then, move on. Stay there as long as you need to but don't set up camp and live there the rest of your life. Move on. Move on into the reality of a silent Holy Saturday where miracles lay brewing, hidden, and sure. Move into the mysterious, ecstatic eruption of Easter morning light. Move toward the "light of life." Seek out the light that overcomes all darkness. And rest there.

I was so moved when my dear friend and her husband left their home and work and traveled across the country to spend a month with their daughter, son-in-law, and grandsons shortly after they received this devastating news. They were grieving, certainly, but also chasing after the gift and joy of new life. Moving toward the light, seeking the light of Christ in their grandsons, in one another, and even in the grieving.

Evil may have its day, but the Lord has won eternity. His word is true. "The light shines in the darkness, and the darkness did not overcome it" (John 1:5). Do you believe it?

It's okay if you don't. I will believe in your stead until, in God's great mercy, your belief is restored to you. Then one day, you can stand in the stead of another who has been profoundly challenged by evil. You can believe for them. You will say to them, "His light shines in the darkness, and evil will not overcome it." And you'll know it's true.

Ponder this before the Lord

Are you struggling to believe that evil will not have the last word? That God's word is true? That he will overcome all darkness? Reach out to someone whose faith is strong and ask them to intercede for you, to believe on your behalf, and then, on your knees, ask the Lord for a renewal of faith, hope, love, and trust in him. He is good.

Closing Epistle

Wait for the LORD;
be strong, and let your heart take courage;
wait for the LORD!
Psalm 27:14

When I travel to offer retreats, I will often open the retreat by asking those in attendance, "Why are you here? What is it that you want? What grace are you hoping to receive?" Jesus asks us all, like he asks blind Bartimaeus in Mark's Gospel, "What do you want me to do for you?" (Mark 10:51). It helps sometimes if we can be specific with the Lord, and name that grace we need. "Lord, I need *this*."

Gifts and graces from the Lord can be funny things with lives all their own—unpredictable, arriving on their own schedule, and sometimes in surprising volume, color, or character. If you opened this book with some expectation, with a hope that you would receive some specific grace, and you find that though you have reached the end, you haven't received that grace yet, that's okay. It doesn't mean you've done anything wrong—that you have failed or that your prayer is ineffective or that Jesus will not grace you. Sometimes we need to wait—to wait for the Lord. He has his reasons for delay. Delay does not mean denial or indifference. Sometimes graces can drop in on us out of nowhere—months or even years after we have asked for them.

And sometimes we have received grace, an abundance of grace, but we just don't perceive it yet. Keep your heart open to the possibility that Jesus has graced you—he is actively inside you, growing new life in you, new healing, even now, even though you cannot perceive it. Like a woman who is newly pregnant, she may not feel that new life inside her for some time. Consider, you might be in a season of early gestation.

Be patient. The Lord knows your need. Better than you do. And he will never forget you.

In the meantime, practice being Bartimaeus. Imagine yourself sitting on the side of the road when a large crowd approaches. You learn that Jesus is among them. Don't be afraid. Cry out to him, "Jesus, Son of David, have mercy on me!"

Ignore any resistance that comes up, any voice that tells you, "He doesn't care about you" or, "He is too busy to listen to you" or, "Who do you think you are crying out to the Lord?" Cry out, again and again. "Son of David, have mercy on me!"

Then allow the Lord, in all of his power and tenderness, to call you to him. Hear him when he speaks these words to your heart, "What do you want me to do for you?"

When Jesus asks us, we need never be afraid of honestly answering this question.

Remember, the beginning of the answer to all you need is already waiting for you in God's word, living and active, awake and attentive to your heart.

September 29, 2025
Feast of the Archangels

Appendix: Rosary of the Holy Wounds

This devotion to the Holy Wounds and the promises were revealed by Our Lord to Sr. Mary Martha Chambon (1841–1907) of the Monastery of the Visitation of Chambery. The cause for her beatification was introduced in 1937. It is customary to honor the five wounds of Our Lord on the five decades.

Prayers: On the crucifix and first three beads:

O JESUS, Divine Redeemer, be merciful to us and to the whole world. Amen.

STRONG God, holy God, immortal God, have mercy on us and on the whole world. Amen.

GRACE and mercy, O my Jesus, during present dangers; cover us with Your Precious Blood. Amen.

ETERNAL Father, grant us mercy through the Blood of Jesus Christ, Your only Son; grant us mercy, we beseech You. Amen, Amen, Amen.

The following prayers, composed by Our Lord, are to be said using the Rosary beads.

On the large [middle] beads:

Eternal Father, I offer You the Wounds of our Lord Jesus Christ.

R/To heal the wounds of our souls.

On the small [decade] beads:

My Jesus, pardon and mercy.

R/Through the merits of Your Holy Wounds.

Closing prayer: Lord Jesus, Man of Sorrows, we have meditated upon **your suffering. We have considered those wounds we know and those unknown to us, and with confidence in your mercy, we ask you to grant us a greater purity of heart, true humility, and courage in our own suffering. We place ourselves and our loved ones into your holy wounds, trusting in your compassion and healing grace. Make us holy and worthy to call you Lord. AMEN.**

Promises of Our Lord for Those Who Practice This Devotion

1. At each word that you pronounce of the Rosary of the Holy Wounds, I allow a drop of My Blood to fall upon the soul of a sinner.

2. Each time that you offer to My Father the merits of My Divine Wounds, you win an immense fortune.

3. Souls that will have contemplated and honored My crown of thorns on earth will be My crown of glory in Heaven!

4. I will grant all that is asked of Me through the invocation of My Holy Wounds. You will obtain everything, because it is through the merit of My Blood, which is of infinite price. With My Wounds and My Divine Heart, everything can be obtained.

5. From My Wounds proceed fruits of sanctity. As gold purified in the crucible becomes more beautiful, so you must put your soul and those of your companions into My sacred Wounds; there they will become perfected as gold in the furnace. You can always purify yourself in My Wounds.

6. My Wounds will repair yours. My Wounds will cover all your faults. Those who honor them will have a true knowledge of Jesus Christ. In meditation on them, you will always find a new love. My Wounds will cover all your sins.

7. Plunge your actions into My Wounds and they will be of value. All your actions, even the least, soaked in My Blood, will acquire by this alone an infinite merit and will please My Heart.

8. In offering My Wounds for the conversion of sinners, even though the sinners are not converted, you will have the same merit before God as if they were.

9. When you have some trouble, something to suffer, quickly place it in My Wounds, and the pain will be alleviated.

10. This aspiration must often be repeated near the sick: "My Jesus, pardon and mercy through the merits of Thy Holy Wounds!" This prayer will solace soul and body.

11. A sinner who will say the following prayer will obtain conversion: "Eternal Father, I offer You the Wounds of our Lord Jesus Christ to heal those of our souls."

12. There will be no death for the soul that expires in My Holy Wounds; they give true life.

13. This rosary is a counterpoise to My justice; it restrains My vengeance.

14. Those who pray with humility and who meditate on My Passion will one day participate in the glory of My Divine Wounds.

15. The more you will have contemplated My painful Wounds on this earth, the higher will be your contemplation of them glorious in Heaven.

16. The soul who during life has honored the Wounds of our Lord Jesus Christ and has offered them to the Eternal Father for the Souls in Purgatory will be accompanied at the moment of death by the Holy Virgin and the Angels; and Our Lord on the Cross, all brilliant in glory, will receive her and crown her.

17. The invocations of the Holy Wounds will obtain an incessant victory for the Church.

*For prayer cards of the Rosary of the Holy Wounds, visit LizK.org.

Notes

[1]   Pope Benedict XVI, T*he Yes of Jesus Christ: Spiritual Exercises in Faith, Hope, and Love* (New York: The Crossroad Publishing Company, 1991), 56, emphasis mine.

[2]   G. K. Chesterton, *St. Thomas Aquinas: The Dumb Ox* (New York: Image Books, 1956), 5.

[3]   Carthusian Monks of the Fourteenth to Seventeenth Centuries, *Ancient Devotions to the Sacred Heart of Jesus* (Herefordshire, UK: Gracewing, 2018), see 53-54.

[4]   Ibid., 62.

The Word Among Us publishes a monthly devotional magazine, books, Bible studies, and pamphlets that help Catholics grow in their faith.

To learn more about who we are and what we publish, visit www.wau.org. There you will find a variety of Catholic resources that will help you grow in your faith.

Your review makes a difference! If you enjoyed this book, please consider sharing your review on Amazon using the QR code below.

www.wau.org